IT'S TIME TO LEARN ABOUT WORLD WAR 2

It's Time to Learn about World War 2

Walter the Educator

Silent King Books
A WhichHead Entertainment Imprint

Copyright © 2024 by Walter the Educator

All rights reserved. No part of this book may be reproduced in any manner whatsoever without written permission except in the case of brief quotations embodied in critical articles and reviews.

First Printing, 2024

Disclaimer

The author and publisher offer this information without warranties expressed or implied. No matter the grounds, neither the author nor the publisher will be accountable for any losses, injuries, or other damages caused by the reader's use of this book. Your use of this book acknowledges an understanding and acceptance of this disclaimer.

It's Time to Learn about World War 2 is a collectible little learning book by Walter the Educator that belongs to the Little Learning Books Series. Collect them all and more books at WaltertheEducator.com

WORLD WAR 2

World War II: A Comprehensive Overview
World War II (1939-1945) remains the most devastating conflict in human history, involving over 30 countries and resulting in an estimated 70-85 million deaths. This global conflict not only reshaped political boundaries but also ushered in significant technological, social, and economic changes that continue to influence the modern world. Understanding World War II requires examining the complex factors that led to its outbreak, the major events of the war, the consequences of the conflict, and its long-lasting impact on international relations and society.

It's Time to Learn about World War 2

Causes of World War II

The Treaty of Versailles and Economic Instability

The Treaty of Versailles, signed in 1919, officially ended World War I, but its harsh terms on Germany laid the groundwork for future conflict. The treaty imposed severe reparations, territorial losses, and military restrictions on Germany, fostering a sense of humiliation and resentment among its population. The economic consequences of these reparations, combined with the global Great Depression in the 1930s, caused widespread poverty and unemployment in Germany, creating fertile ground for extremist ideologies.

It's Time to Learn about World War 2

The Rise of Totalitarian Regimes
During the interwar years, several nations saw the rise of totalitarian regimes that promised to restore national pride and reverse economic hardship. In Germany, Adolf Hitler and the Nazi Party rose to power by exploiting national discontent, promoting anti-Semitic propaganda, and promising to undo the Treaty of Versailles. Italy, under Benito Mussolini, also embraced fascism, while Japan pursued militarism under the rule of Emperor Hirohito and his advisors. These regimes shared common goals of expansionism, nationalism, and authoritarian control, which set the stage for aggressive actions in the late 1930s.

It's Time to Learn about World War 2

Expansionism and Appeasement
The 1930s saw aggressive territorial expansion by totalitarian regimes. Japan invaded Manchuria in 1931 and launched a full-scale invasion of China in 1937. Italy invaded Ethiopia in 1935, seeking to build a new Roman Empire. Germany, under Hitler, began a series of territorial conquests, including the remilitarization of the Rhineland (1936), the annexation of Austria (1938), and the seizure of Czechoslovakia's Sudetenland (1938). The Western democracies, particularly Britain and France, pursued a policy of appeasement, believing that concessions could prevent another large-scale war. However, this only emboldened Hitler and other dictators, leading to further aggression.

It's Time to Learn about World War 2

The Invasion of Poland
The immediate cause of World War II was Germany's invasion of Poland on September 1, 1939. Hitler sought to regain lost territories and expand Germany's influence in Eastern Europe.

It's Time to Learn about World War 2

In response to the invasion, Britain and France, which had guaranteed Polish independence, declared war on Germany on September 3, 1939. Despite these declarations, Poland fell quickly due to the overwhelming strength of the German military, marking the beginning of a conflict that would soon engulf the entire world.

It's Time to Learn about World War 2

Major Events of World War II
The Early Phase (1939-1941)
The early years of World War II were dominated by the rapid success of German military tactics, particularly blitzkrieg (lightning war).

It's Time to Learn about World War 2

This strategy relied on the swift movement of tanks, infantry, and air power to overwhelm enemies and capture territory quickly. After the fall of Poland, Germany turned its attention to Western Europe, invading Denmark and Norway in April 1940.

It's Time to Learn about World War 2

In May 1940, German forces launched a major offensive in the west, quickly defeating Belgium, the Netherlands, and Luxembourg, before invading France. By June 1940, France had fallen, and Germany controlled much of Western Europe.

It's Time to Learn about World War 2

The Battle of Britain (1940) marked a critical turning point. After France's defeat, Germany sought to neutralize Britain through aerial bombardment.

It's Time to Learn about World War 2

However, the British Royal Air Force successfully defended the nation, and Germany's invasion plans were abandoned. Britain remained a crucial base of operations for the Allies throughout the war.

It's Time to Learn about World War 2

In the Pacific, Japan sought to expand its empire by invading territories across East and Southeast Asia. The invasion of China, which began in 1937, was part of a broader strategy to establish dominance in the region and secure resources for Japan's industrial and military needs.

It's Time to Learn about World War 2

The Widening of the Conflict (1941-1942)
In June 1941, Germany launched Operation Barbarossa, the largest military invasion in history, against the Soviet Union. Hitler's goal was to conquer the Soviet Union, eliminate communism, and secure vast natural resources. Initially, the Germans made significant advances, but they were unprepared for the harsh Russian winter and the determined Soviet resistance. The Battle of Moscow in December 1941 marked the first major defeat for the German army.

It's Time to Learn about World War 2

On December 7, 1941, Japan launched a surprise attack on the United States at Pearl Harbor, Hawaii. This event led to the U.S. entry into World War II, transforming the conflict into a truly global war.

It's Time to Learn about World War 2

In response, the United States declared war on Japan, and Germany and Italy, as Japan's allies, declared war on the U.S. This brought the full industrial and military might of the United States into the conflict, which would prove decisive in the war's outcome.

It's Time to Learn about World War 2

The Turning Points (1942-1943)
Several key battles in 1942-1943 marked the turning points of World War II, shifting the momentum in favor of the Allies.

It's Time to Learn about World War 2

The Battle of Stalingrad (1942-1943): One of the most significant and brutal battles of the war took place in the Soviet city of Stalingrad. German forces, seeking to capture the city and secure control over the oil fields of the Caucasus, engaged in fierce urban warfare with Soviet troops.

It's Time to Learn about World War 2

Despite heavy casualties, the Soviet Red Army encircled and defeated the German 6th Army in February 1943. The Battle of Stalingrad was a major turning point on the Eastern Front, marking the beginning of the German retreat.

It's Time to Learn about World War 2

The Battle of Midway (June 1942): In the Pacific, the Battle of Midway was a critical naval engagement between the United States and Japan.

It's Time to Learn about World War 2

The U.S. Navy, under the command of Admiral Chester W. Nimitz, successfully ambushed and sank four Japanese aircraft carriers. This victory crippled Japan's naval power and halted its expansion in the Pacific, shifting the balance of power in favor of the Allies.

It's Time to Learn about World War 2

The North African Campaign (1940-1943): In North Africa, the Allies, led by British General Bernard Montgomery and American General Dwight D. Eisenhower, achieved a decisive victory over the German and Italian forces led by General Erwin Rommel (the "Desert Fox") at the Battle of El Alamein in 1942. The success in North Africa allowed the Allies to invade Italy in 1943, leading to the eventual fall of Mussolini's fascist regime.

It's Time to Learn about World War 2

The Allied Offensive (1944-1945)
By 1944, the Allies had gained the upper hand in both Europe and the Pacific. In June 1944, the Allies launched Operation Overlord, commonly known as D-Day, with a massive amphibious assault on the beaches of Normandy, France. Led by General Eisenhower, this operation marked the beginning of the liberation of Western Europe from Nazi control. Paris was liberated in August 1944, and the Allies continued their advance toward Germany.

It's Time to Learn about World War 2

In the Pacific, the U.S. adopted a strategy of "island hopping," capturing key islands to establish bases closer to Japan. The battles of Iwo Jima (February-March 1945) and Okinawa (April-June 1945) were particularly brutal and demonstrated Japan's fierce resistance.

It's Time to Learn about World War 2

The United States also used its superior industrial capacity to produce large numbers of ships, planes, and weapons, overwhelming Japan's ability to sustain the war effort.

It's Time to Learn about World War 2

The End of the War in Europe
By early 1945, the Allies were closing in on Germany from both the east and west. Soviet forces captured Berlin in May 1945, and Hitler, facing inevitable defeat, committed suicide in his bunker on April 30, 1945.

It's Time to Learn about World War 2

On May 8, 1945, Germany officially surrendered to the Allies, marking the end of World War II in Europe. This day is known as V-E Day (Victory in Europe Day).

It's Time to Learn about World War 2

The End of the War in the Pacific
Despite the defeat of Germany, the war in the Pacific continued. The United States, under President Harry S. Truman, sought to bring the war to a swift conclusion. After fierce fighting in the Pacific and the refusal of Japan to surrender, the U.S. dropped two atomic bombs on the Japanese cities of Hiroshima (August 6, 1945) and Nagasaki (August 9, 1945).

It's Time to Learn about World War 2

The unprecedented destruction caused by these bombs, combined with the Soviet Union's declaration of war on Japan, led to Japan's surrender on August 15, 1945. This day is known as V-J Day (Victory over Japan Day), and World War II officially ended.

It's Time to Learn about World War 2

Consequences of World War II
The Human Cost
World War II was the deadliest conflict in human history, with an estimated 70-85 million people killed. This staggering death toll includes soldiers and civilians, with millions perishing in battles, bombings, and atrocities. The Holocaust, perpetrated by Nazi Germany, resulted in the systematic murder of six million Jews, as well as millions of others, including Romani people, disabled individuals, political dissidents, and LGBTQ+ individuals. The war also saw widespread destruction of cities, infrastructure, and industries, particularly in Europe and Asia.

It's Time to Learn about World War 2

The Cold War and the Division of Europe
In the aftermath of World War II, the geopolitical landscape shifted dramatically. The United States and the Soviet Union emerged as the two superpowers, with vastly different political ideologies—capitalism

It's Time to Learn about World War 2

and democracy versus communism and authoritarianism. This ideological divide led to the Cold War, a period of intense rivalry and tension between the Western bloc (led by the U.S.) and the Eastern bloc (led by the Soviet Union). Europe was divided along these lines, with Eastern Europe falling under Soviet influence and Western Europe aligning with the U.S. and its allies. Germany itself was split into two countries: West Germany (Federal Republic of Germany) and East Germany (German Democratic Republic), with the city of Berlin symbolizing the division.

It's Time to Learn about World War 2

The United Nations and International Cooperation
World War II also led to the establishment of the United Nations (UN) in 1945. The UN was created to promote international peace and security, prevent future conflicts, and foster cooperation among nations. Unlike its predecessor, the League of Nations, the UN included the world's major powers, including the U.S., the Soviet Union, China, the United Kingdom, and France, which formed the core of the Security Council. The creation of the UN marked a new era of multilateral diplomacy and international cooperation.

It's Time to Learn about World War 2

The Economic Impact and Reconstruction
The economic impact of World War II was profound. Europe and Asia faced massive reconstruction efforts, as cities, industries, and infrastructure had been destroyed. The U.S. implemented the Marshall Plan, a large-scale economic aid program to help rebuild Europe and prevent the spread of communism. Japan, under American occupation, underwent a significant transformation, adopting democratic reforms and rebuilding its economy to become a global economic power by the 1960s.

It's Time to Learn about World War 2

The war also marked the beginning of the end for colonial empires. In the years following World War II, many countries in Asia, Africa, and the Middle East gained independence from European colonial powers, leading to the process of decolonization.

It's Time to Learn about World War 2

Technological and Social Changes
Technological Advancements

World War II was a period of rapid technological innovation. The development of radar, jet engines, and advanced medical treatments, such as antibiotics, transformed both military and civilian life. The war also accelerated research into nuclear energy, culminating in the development of the atomic bomb by the United States. The post-war era saw the beginnings of the nuclear arms race between the U.S. and the Soviet Union, which would shape global politics for decades.

It's Time to Learn about World War 2

Social and Cultural Shifts

The war also had a significant impact on social and cultural norms. In many countries, women entered the workforce in large numbers to fill roles left vacant by men who were serving in the military. This shift challenged traditional gender roles and laid the groundwork for the women's rights movements of the 1960s and beyond. Additionally, the war exposed the horrors of racism, xenophobia, and totalitarianism, leading to a global reckoning with issues of human rights and justice.

It's Time to Learn about World War 2

The Nuremberg Trials (1945-1946) were held to bring Nazi war criminals to justice, establishing the principle of individual accountability for crimes against humanity and setting a precedent for future international tribunals.

It's Time to Learn about World War 2

Conclusion

World War II was a transformative event in world history, reshaping nations, economies, and ideologies. Its causes, rooted in unresolved tensions from World War I and the rise of totalitarian regimes, led to a global conflict of unprecedented scale. The war's major events, including the battles in Europe and the Pacific, the Holocaust, and the use of atomic weapons, had far-reaching consequences for international relations, political systems, and technological advancements.

The legacy of World War II is still felt today in the form of international institutions like the United Nations, the division of Europe during the Cold War, and the ongoing challenges of preventing global conflict. Understanding World War II is essential for comprehending the modern world and the lessons learned from one of the darkest periods in human history.

ABOUT THE CREATOR

Walter the Educator is one of the pseudonyms for Walter Anderson. Formally educated in Chemistry, Business, and Education, he is an educator, an author, a diverse entrepreneur, and he is the son of a disabled war veteran. "Walter the Educator" shares his time between educating and creating. He holds interests and owns several creative projects that entertain, enlighten, enhance, and educate, hoping to inspire and motivate you. Follow, find new works, and stay up to date with Walter the Educator™ at WaltertheEducator.com

www.ingramcontent.com/pod-product-compliance
Lightning Source LLC
LaVergne TN
LVHW051926060526
838201LV00062B/4700